TRUMPINGTON

98/165

To Carol with very best wishes

Tim Kerslaw

TRUMPINGTON THE OWL

Tim Kershaw

victoria press

Author's note: *Bringing up the Ammunition* was written after reading *A Subaltern's Odyssey - A Memoir of the Great War 1915-17* by R.B. Talbot Kelly, my school art teacher.

ISBN 0 907165 22 2

© Victoria Press 1989

Poems copyright © Tim Kershaw

Illustrations, p. 22, 31, 39, 40
copyright © Gloria Bousfield

Illustrations, p. 20, 23, 29 (drawn photo), 38
copyright © Alan Robinson

Illustration: owl clutching dog
copyright © Tim Kershaw

First published in 1989 by Victoria Press,
50 Buckland Road, Maidstone, Kent ME16 0SH.
(Tel: 0622-52656)

Distributed by Meresborough Books,
17 Station Road, Rainham, Kent ME8 7RS.
(Tel: 0634-388812)

Typeset and designed by The River Press,
Maidstone, Kent.

Printed and bound in Great Britain by
Antony Rowe Ltd, Bumper's Farm,
Chippenham SN14 6LH.

Contents

Trumpington the Owl

I had an owl called Trumpington.
I kept him in my loo.
The size was almost right for him,
Six foot by four foot two.

He nested in the basin
(Plug removed for sanitation)
And I got the local mason in
To make an alteration

To the ventilator grille
So that it would fit the bill
As a sally-port for Trumpington
When he went out to kill.

It took a while to train him
But I'm happy to report
That Trumpington was by and large
A pretty studious sort.

He learned what I required of him
In two months and a week.
I clipped his claws each Thursday night.
I sharpened up his beak.

I sharpened up his appetite
With mouse and sparrow flan
Until at last he was prepared
To implement my plan.

Now my neighbour, Mrs Wadkin,
Was a terrible old cow,
But I'd treated her politely
and discreetly up till now.

She was gossipy and tiresome,
Inquisitive and mean,
Knew what was best for people
And could frequently be seen

Observing through lace curtains
From her special window seat
The goings-on of everyone
Inhabiting her street.

She kept a frightful yapping dog,
A sort of compromise
of poodle and chihuaha
With a Yorkshire terrier's eyes

Which she doted on and tarted up
And spoiled and overfed.
It dressed in tartan overcoats.
It even shared her bed.

I don't know which I hated most,
The way it yapped and howled
Or the way that my new garden path
Was regularly fouled.

One Saturday, I reckoned,
It was time for satisfaction,
So I briefed old Trumpers carefully
and girt his loins for action

And when at last the milkman came
And rang my neighbour's bell
I crouched behind her dustbins
And I gave a fearsome yell.

The dreadful dog she doted on
Came yapping to my feet
While Trumpington looked down on it,
Just waiting for his treat.

I stood and gave the signal
When the milkman's call was done
And Trumpington came plummeting,
Claws gleaming in the sun.

He snatched the wretched mongrel up.
He took off like a lift
While wingeing Mrs Wadkin stood
And shivered in her shift,

Stood open-mouthed and horrified,
Too shocked to shout or shriek
As she watched the final, fatal flight
Of her frightful furry freak.

Trumpers circled lazily
Then headed for the east,
Still clutching on the creature
Who would be his evening feast.

They grew gradually smaller,
They were just a silhouette,
Until at last they vanished,
Hidden by a passing jet.

Mrs Wadkin's anger
Was so great she couldn't speak.
She's gone and bought a vulture.
The return match is next week.

The Ostrich

Do not feed
The ostrich bird
Because, in case
You hadn't heard,
His appetite
Is quite absurd.

He rather fancies
Curious things
Like rusty tins
And sofa springs
And broken glass
And wedding rings.

He'll gobble down
With obvious greed
Old nuts and bolts
And budgie seed
Mixed up with lumps
of concrete screed.

He'll stop at naught,
This fearsome fowl:
A hairbrush or
A builder's trowel
Are grist to his
Well-armoured bowel.

Discretion is,
I promise you,
The better part
Of valour. Do
Not feed him or
He'll have you too.

The Sheep

You all know the sheep:
She's a dopey, half-asleep
Sort of creature with a bathmat on her back
And a long, stupid face
With a large empty space
Between her ears, and a quite amazing knack
Of suddenly revealing
She's as great a depth of feeling
As a half-rotten gatepost or an old potato sack.

The Day of the Camel

My camel's name was Abdul.
I bought him from a man
Who called one day and chanced to say
He had one in his van.

I said, "You must be joking!"
I entertained some doubt.
So he replied, "Hang on a jiff,
I'll get the fellow out."

So I stood there on my doorstep and
I watched with some alarm.
The wretched man unlocked his van.
There stood, devoid of charm,

A creature so disdainful,
So haughty and so proud.
"He's what you need," the man declared,
"To stand out from the crowd."

"I rather think," I tried to say,
"I'd look a real berk.
Do I park him on the meter
When I've ridden him to work?"

"Come off it, squire," the man replied.
I said, "I think I would.
I don't know how to ride one
And I wouldn't if I could."

"This camel's not for riding,"
Said the man with some dismay,
"He's a camel with a pedigree,
The kind that you display.

That's why his coat's so beautiful,
All pom-poms, curls and tufts.
He's going to be the champion
At this year's camel Crufts.

His old man's pretty posh,
The only camel in Debretts.
The whole world knows his portrait,
It's on Camel cigarettes.

His grandad came from Scotland -
You've heard of Camel Laird -
And his air ace uncle Sopwith
Left no hun unspared.

A still more distant ancestor
Achieved his share of fame
By helping out King Arthur -
He gave Camelot its name.

And turning to his mother's side,
From which he got his hump,
She was Florence of Arabia,
The Lady with the Lump."

"I must say, you've convinced me.
I'm incredibly impressed.
A camel with his ancestry
Must be the very best.

So how about, say, seven quid?"
(I said it just for fun).
The man looked down and thought a bit,
Then suddenly said "Done!"

That's how I got my camel.
I led the beast inside
And thought "Have I been taken
For a lousy camel ride?"

I sat and stared at Abdul.
I pondered what to do,
And then a brainwave hit me
And I phoned the local zoo.

They said, "We have no room for him.
Our camel quota's full.
Why don't you try the craft shop?
They might take him for his wool."

I think the camel overheard.
He got up on his feet,
Knocked down the door and galloped off
Along my narrow street,

Neck stretched straight in front of him,
Ears back, with heaving hump,
Not so much a gallop as
A lolloping gallump.

He raced along the High Street
(It was early closing day)
When suddenly he stopped. He'd heard
Some music far away.

He screeched around the corner, then
Ground to a sudden stop.
The tune he heard was coming from
A circus's big top.

He trotted right into the ring,
His gaze set straight ahead.
He trotted to the man he sought,
A man dressed all in red.

"It's nice to see old Abdul back"
(it was the boss who spoke).
"Some moron went and nicked him,
Some kind of stupid joke.

Thanks a lot for saving him,
I feared he'd gone abroad.
Oh, and while I think of it,
Here's seven quid reward."

My Old Croc

A crocodile's giving me problems.
He appeared in my bath in the night.
He was really quite small, an inch or two tall,
But he gave me a terrible fright.

He must have come up through the plughole.
I fed him on eggs and pork pies.
He first said hello a good fortnight ago;
Since then he has doubled in size.

His character's odd. He's quite friendly,
At least when I offer him food.
Most of the time he's more happy than snappy
But sometimes he'll just lie and brood.

There are some things that really annoy him,
Like not having doughnuts for tea,
But sometimes he'll watch Noel Edmunds,
Curled up and all snug on my knee.

Lately he's taken to roaming,
Just like a cat on the prowl.
He's brought me dead chickens and pigeons
And other things equally foul.

It seems he eats anything yellow,
Custard and lemon curd tarts.
Today he was chomping bananas and daffs.
It's dreadful whenever he starts

To attack the object he's chosen,
So I got him a collar and lead
And went out in the park (it was well before dark).
He stopped by a lamp-post and freed

Himself from his tether so quickly
I didn't have time to exclaim
He went like greased lightning. I think something
     frightning
Had scared him. He wasn't to blame.

A fat traffic warden was booking
A car at a meter nearby.
He got in a flap when the croc ate his cap
And then started gnawing his thigh.

I jumped and I grabbed but I missed him.
He slipped through my hands and was gone.
No good to explain to the warden in pain,
Who was looking exceedingly wan.

Then the croc slipped down a grating
And utterly vanished from view.

I went home and filled up a bath to relax.
Through the plughole I heard him: "Yoohoo!"

Cross-Channel Lemur

My Aunt, who was something of a dreamer,
Met a lemur on a cross-channel steamer.

She became aware of its presence
When it terrified six Breton peasants
By shouting out loud from the rigging
Fierce blood-curdling oaths, then dewigging
James Justice QC, who happened to be
In the forward saloon taking crumpets for tea.

My Aunt wasn't very nonplussed.
She knew that friendship and trust
Were things that all creatures respected.
The lemur, she knew, felt rejected.

So she started to talk
The beast down from its perch
When all of a sudden
The ship gave a lurch.

Straight into her arms
With a cry it descended.
It was cuddled and petted
And spoiled and befriended.

But the creature my Aunt had believed was a friend
Stole her bag and ran off when they docked at Ostend.

The Gecko

God gave the gecko
Swivelling eyes
So it can have a dekko
At the flies.

Champagne Tree

How I would like to be
A champagne tree.
I would blow bubbles
And get pissed as a newt
And shoot corks at people
Who tried to steal my fruit.

Opting Out

I'm sitting in the sunshine
in a field full of flowers.
I feel warm, relaxed and drowsy.
I could linger here for hours.

Some people say I'm opting out.
I sit here with my gin.
This is what it's all about.
Stuff your opting in.

The Electrician

He was a live wire.
She turned him on.
His eyes lit up
When he saw her.
The neighbours were shocked
When they connected.
Their lives fused.
They went out together.

Living on the Coast

There were ferries at the bottom of my garden
but now there's bloody hovercraft too.

Graymalkin Rides

The woods outside are dark and still,
A silver frost lies on the hill,
Nothing moves and nothing will -
   Graymalkin rides tonight.

Everywhere let doors be barred!
Everyone, be on your guard!
The night is long, the night is hard -
   Graymalkin rides tonight.

Windows closed and curtains drawn
Will shield you from Graymalkin's scorn.
Stay at home until the dawn!
   Graymalkin rides tonight.

Everyone must heed my verse,
For I have known Graymalkin's curse.
I warn you all, from in my hearse -
   Graymalkin rides tonight!

Gossip Column

A grotty young pop star props up the bar,
Telling a bored-looking chaperone
About his new radio telephone
And how the thing works in his car.

Lurking behind a column I hear:
"Our eldest is now in the Guards, my dear,
And my gilts are well below par."

Smooth merchant bankers loudly complain:
"The champagne's too warm." "Too flat." "Too sweet."
A gaggle of Sloanes nurse aching feet,
Their faces contorted with pain.

Still behind my column, I hear:
"Anthea's gone to Zermatt this year
In Prince What's-his-name's new private plane."

A developer says, looking bored as hell:
"He's a clot to go on a yacht that's not
Equipped with a loo. A chamber pot
Is all very well, but in a swell . . ."

I leave my column, mildly pissed,
Smile at a passing columnist
And say: "I've got NEWS. I'll sell."

La Napoule, April

The Cote d'Azur is grey today,
Wet with rain and wet with spray.
The Frenchman hurries on his way,
The tourists here regret their stay.

The lights are on in every room
But nothing can dispel the gloom.
The waves keep on their sullen boom,
The flowers as yet refuse to bloom.

A sudden roar, a train goes by
Belching smoke to soil the sky.
The clouds are low, the hills are high,
The tourists curse and mutter "Why?

"Why did we come abroad this year?
Why must we pay so much for beer?
Why, oh why, won't the weather clear?
Why on earth did we all come here?

"Why are the hotel rooms so damp?
No wonder that we've all got cramp.
Why has the lounge only got one lamp?
Why didn't we go to a holiday camp?

"My God, what an awful holiday!
But if it's so bad, why do we stay?"

Clouds

I.   Laprade

I sat in a field full of orchids.
There was only one cloud to be seen.
It was small, it was puffy and far, far away,
Incredibly white, pure and clean.

II.   Toulouse

I sat in a jam on the by-pass.
There was only one cloud. It was mean.
It was yellow and heavy, it stank of old eggs
And utterly ruined the scene.

Dawn, Tuscany

Machiavellian castles rise
From sullied soil to starry skies,
Then glisten in new-morning haze,
With rising sun take on new guise.

Soon noble stand in jagged shapes,
With bitter past like Tuscan grapes;
Devoid of confidence and hopes,
In each a dismal portal gapes,

Reminding of mediaeval host,
Kingdoms stretched from coast to coast;
Warlike kingdoms later lost
In spite of vain Medici boast.

Memories of treasure turned
To dust and all save buildings burned.

Poetry Reading 1968

We read aloud from Owen and Sassoon,
Graves, Grenfell, Seeger, Rosenberg and Brooke.
A good two dozen people sat and listened
As we reminded them how war might look.

We read our poems at the British Council
In a peaceful, sun-steeped city by the sea.
Such slaughter seemed so distant in Beirut.

Bringing up the Ammunition

Flanders 1916

Me with the ammo pack
Deep in the mud and black
Slogging along the track
Up to my knees.

No moon to give us light,
Battery way out of sight.
Get there and back tonight
God if you please.

Shrapnel rounds rend the air
Crumple and bend the air
Deafening everywhere
Hammer and thud.

Blown off my feet again,
Nearby a howl of pain.
Never see him again,
Drowned in the mud.

Slip again, stand and yell
"Mick and Bert! Where the hell
Are you all? I can't tell!
Give us a light!"

No chance they'll hear me, though,
Shells are too near me, so
Rigid with fear we go
On through the night.

Suddenly, right ahead,
Glimmering light ahead,
Gun pit in sight ahead,
Mick and Bert too.

Unload the ammo case,
Time to head back to base,
Back through that dreadful place.
God see us through!

Car Crash

Death almost caught me.
I drove warily through the snow,
Unaware of his presence,
Crisping along the carriageway.

He came suddenly,
Disguised as a stationery car.
I swerved and missed
But he slipped ice under my wheels,

Sent me skeetering headlong,
Drew me across the reservation,
Bore down on me, horn blaring,
Laughed as glass splintered.

In a wrenching tangle of metal
He dropped me against the embankment
But I stepped into the cold night
Mocking his efforts.

I shouted defiance,
Strode to the ambulance.
A routine check, said the nurse.
Death entered my body and chuckled,

Tore at my guts, bleared my brain,
Drank my blood lustily,
Froze my limbs with his breath.
My mind reeled. My teeth clenched.

They laid me out, gassed me, operated.
Death slunk away.
I woke and smiled again,
Exulted, but quietly.

The Hare

I was walking not far from home.
I saw, suddenly,
something I'd not seen for years.

A hare,
sitting half upright,
ears high, alert as a sentry,
front paws poised,
sniffing the April air.

The hare was poised in a glass case,
frozen in death,
in a shop window,
for sale.

Crooked Sally

Sally has a crooked face.
She's rising seventeen.
Her upper lip is hardly there,
The lower sticks out, full and square,
Her chin looks big and mean.

One eye is straight,
The other's drooped.
Her longing soul is hurdled, cooped
Inside her twisted features.
In other ways she's just the same
As any other teenage frame,
Another of God's creatures.

A twist of fate, a twist of face,
Had made her future grim.
However much she longs to kiss
The boy across the street, such bliss
He's certain to refuse her:
At least until the boy grows up
And learns a face is just a cup
Containing wine that's sweet or sour;
A mis-shaped vase may hold a flower.
If he could see her inner grace,
If she could make it clear to him
It's certain he would choose her.

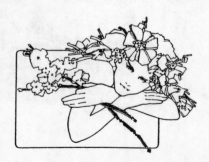

Chancery Lane

A man at the window across the street
parts the curtain furtively,
sniffing the outside air.

A small lock-up shop below
sells vivid green cardigans with green stamps.
No one goes in.

Next door a jeweller's window glistens with garnets,
engagement rings by the score.
Girls gaze longingly every day.
They never buy.

There's the barbers. "Hairdressing, Chiropody"
says the sign.
If you took your socks off they'd be horrified.

The paper man sells the "Stannud"
and "Revally" occasionally.
He hasn't shouted the headlines in years.

The cigarette shop is a dark cavern.
Old Jack blinks in the dimness;
his only overheads are 25 watts.

Steel-shuttered vaults under the street,
rich as Aladdin with silver.
Wrapped when it's bought, it never sees daylight.

The bookshop down the cold, dank basement steps
says "Back Soon" on the door.
The sign looks pre-war.

The sun shines overhead,
but several stories up.

Hambledon Hill

We stood minutely, humbled by Hambledon:
grass far above us, trees in the clouds.
We strode, walked, slowed and clambered,
clumped upward,
tramping the mud of our footway.

Field of flintstone, pebble-dash hillside
stretched onward, scraping the dusk.
We walked to the edge of the world,
where we gasped at the blast of the air's icy purity,
found us on high, mastering countryscape
saw the horizon all round us.

Dusk fell on us spellbound.
We turned as the pall of the night
swept up the valley,
headed on homeward,
afraid to be eyeless on Hambledon.
Dwarfed in the darkness, we stumbled and wept
as wind whipped our faces, trapped in the void.

We scurried and skeltered the slope of the hillside,
slid lower and downward, came to the car,
its warmth and containment;
gazed at the stark hill darkening.

Lights stab the blackness,
homeward road beckons.
How vast is Hambledon?
Our car can surround it in seconds,
so humble is Hambledon.

Elgar's Cello Concerto

Played by Andrew Lloyd-Webber
at the Albert Hall

He held the cello as tenderly
as the woman he loved.
He cradled her in his bent left arm
with his right hand poised.
The strokes of his bow inspired her strings
and she sang her song.

She sang of anguish and despair
dissolved by joy.
She sang with a passion that overwhelmed
the violins,
a passion that soared with mounting fire
till the air glowed gold,

And as she sang she cast a spell
and I breathed her flame.
My dying embers leapt to life
with a vigour I'd thought was lost
and my spirit shone.

Watching Television

Your lean legs long-lying lay trousered and booted,
stretched straight on the carpet, you watched as you sat.
You sat with an elbow propped up on a footstool,
head lowered and silent, intent as a cat.

Chin resting lightly on gently bent fingers,
hair falling long in a line with your arm;
your dignity, poise and your earnest composure
contrast with their chatter: so raucous: so calm.

They were larger and louder, less lithe, little minded,
with limited outlook and lacking your grace.
They watched the screen while you stared at the embers.
A flame flickered suddenly, lit up your face.

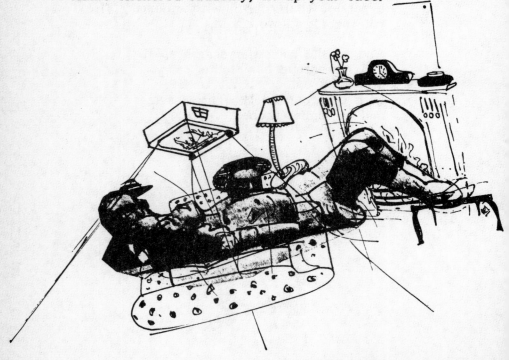

When You Went

I cursed the days that kept us far apart.
You looked into my eyes and saw my heart.

More and More

Is the fact deplorable -
It's surely not ignorable -
I find you more and moreable
Delightful and adorable.

How Did it Happen?

How did it happen? It just happened.
I loved you too dearly; perhaps it frightened you.
Anyway, you wrote, to emphasise the unrequitedness
Of my love that I had felt so long.

We changed, perhaps. Perhaps? No doubt.
Or was it only me who changed?
I wish I knew. I lost you
And despaired.

My passion lessened with the passing weeks
But caught me unaware from time to time,
As now. I write to ease my mind
But time alone can ease it.

Two facts are all I cling to:
I love you; you are gone.

Song: Round and Round

Round and round the record goes,
on and on the music plays.
It fills our eyes with sweet surprise
down all our days.

> *All our days*
> *music plays.*

Round and round the record goes,
on and on the singer sings
of smiles and woes, goodbyes, hellos,
these foolish things.

> *These foolish things*
> *music brings.*

Round and round our memories go,
on and on down all our years,
weaving patterns to and fro
from hopes and fears.

> *Hopes and fears,*
> *smiles and tears.*

Song: the City Paper Seller

For fifty long years I 'ave stood on this spot.
I've met many people, both famous and not.
But in all the long years that I've stood on this street
There's one man I've always been waiting to meet.
I dream of the evening when 'e will come by -
'E'll doff 'is plumed 'at and look me in the eye,
'E'll stand there and smile with 'is gleaming gold chain
And I will start singing again and again:

Lord Mayor, it's so nice to meet you,
I've been longing for the day.
I feel it's such a pity
To be working in the City
And never to 'ave seen you till today.

Now sometimes I wonder what it'd be like
To pack up me papers and say "I'm on strike,
Won't sell no more papers till you City gents
All make me Lord Mayor, and 'ang the expense."
I'd dine off gold plates and smoke massive cigars,
Wear beautiful robes, ride in coaches and cars,
Drink gallons and gallons of port every night
And then I'd start singing with all of me might:

Lord Mayor, what a lovely feeling!
I love wallowing in wine!
I look out on the City
And it all looks very pretty
Especially 'cos I know that it's all mine!

But 'e never comes by, and I wonder if I
Shall see 'im some day 'fore my time comes to die.
I'd give anything to shake 'im by the 'and
And to see 'im stood there by me newspaper stand.
But if 'e came now, after all these long years,
I wouldn't be able to see 'im for tears.
I'm packing up now for to 'ave a few beers
But I'll still practise singing in case 'e appears:

> *Lord Mayor, it's so nice to meet you,*
> *I've been longing for the day.*
> *I feel it's such a pity*
> *To be working in the City*
> *And never to 'ave met you.*

Never.

Song: Middle-Aged Ladies

I dreamed of a man who was loving and witty,
I dreamed of a man who was handsome and strong.
Those were the days when men thought I was pretty,
    Those were the days
        Of laughter and song.

Middle-aged ladies who find life so boring,
Ladies whose children are now fully grown,
Ladies whose husbands are snoring or whoring,
    Ladies who find
        That they're all alone.

I dreamed that my life would be rich and fulfilling,
I dreamed of the sharing of husband and wife.
I was young, I was hopeful and trusting and willing,
    Bound to be happy
        The rest of my life.

Middle-aged ladies with nothing to live for,
Listlessly seeking a purpose, a goal,
Wondering joylessly what they would give for
    Their time again,
        Regaining their soul.

I dream now so little of what once inspired me,
I dream now of treading the long road ahead.
Where are the hopes that once thrilled me and fired me?
        Where have they gone?
        Why have they fled?

Middle-aged ladies, you've married and mothered,
Ladies, that part of your life is now done,
Your youth while you did it was buried and smothered,
    Biding its time:
        Now it's back in the sun.

I'm doing the things now I never had time for,
Found that I'm free now the children are grown,
Indulging in things there's no reason or rhyme for,
        Just to enjoy them . . .
              Dreams of my own.

45

Yuxbridge

Pin-striped zombie
Slaving in the City,
Mainstay of Metroland,
Petty Walter Mitty.

White-faced automaton,
Never sees the sun;
Twilight traveller,
Envies others' fun.

Ovaltine early,
Little time for leisure:
Must be alert at work,
Simulating pleasure.

Cultivates garden,
Pottering for hours.
No place for fruit and veg,
Only pretty flowers.

Selfish, spoilt children.
Grammar school? Some hope.
Housewife, once houseproud,
Valium now to cope.

One day ship come in;
Retire; country cottage.
Too late. Soul destroyed.
What a mess of pottage.

Wisteria Wimple

Of all the nauseous nieces I have known
I think Wisteria Wimple was the worst.
Her eyes were crossed, she looked half lost
and vaguely unrehearsed.

She lived a few doors down the road.
She used to call on me
When coming home from grammar school
And longing for some tea.

I used to give her cakes and scones,
Digestive biscuits, too;
Plates of ham and strawberry jam
And peanut butter goo.

With little gurgling cries of glee
She'd stuff her greedy face
And then with chocolate on her cheeks
She'd go to rinse her brace.

I tolerated her for years,
Her lumpishness and greed,
But thought I'd nip her in the bud
Before she went to seed.

I made an awful chocolate cake
With arsenic inside.
She ate it down with scarce a frown
Then sighed and burped and died.

Things went quiet for several months.
I never even missed her.
Then one day the doorbell rang:
It was her little sister.

Mrs Mary Mattock's Christmas Pud

Mrs Mary Mattock made
A monster Christmas pud
Full of all the things she thought
Were interesting and good.

Apart from all the usual things –
Mixed fruit and candied peel –
There was avocado, aubergine,
Lasagne and smoked eel.

There was celery and tuna quiche,
Duck paté, lemon sole,
Salami, orange sorbet,
After Eights, profiteroles,

Tortillas, guacamolé,
Gazpacho, Dijon mustard,
Half a glass of rosé and
A delicate egg custard.

She mixed them up and put them in
Her biggest pudding dish.
She started stirring with her spoon
And made her Christmas wish.

It didn't taste quite right to her.
She pondered what to do,
Then added curry powder and
An anchovy or two.

She was just about to cook it
When her husband Ron came in,
Late from work and tired and wet,
Demanding instant gin.

"Taste the pudding, darling,
And then I'll mix your drink.
Everything I like's in there.
Just tell me what you think."

So he took the spoon and tried it.
He said, "That's pretty good,
But if you added something more
You'd have a smashing pud.

Some cornflakes and some orange juice
Would add a bit of zest,
Some steak and chips and ketchup
And a pint of Courage Best

And what about some treacle tart?
A double shish kebab?
A chicken in a basket
And fried onions and crab?

A popadum, some lychees
And a bowl of Irish stew?
I reckon if you add that lot
Your Christmas pud will do."

She thought "Now I can cook it"
When her little boy walked in.
"What's for tea, then, Mum?" he said,
"And when can I begin?"

"Taste the pudding first," she said,
"And tell me what you feel,
And when I know just what you think
You'll get your evening meal."

"It isn't bad, Mum, but it needs
A lot of extra things
Like doughnuts and fish fingers
And Heinz spaghetti rings,

Just one cornetto, instant whip
And peanut butter too,
And then you'll have a pudding
That I reckon might just do."

She tried again to cook it
When her neighbour Grace dropped in
With a broken bra strap:
Could she scrounge a safety pin?

"Hang around a little longer,"
Mary told her, "till you've tried
The pudding of the century"
And she glowed with mother's pride.

"Ooh, I'm not sure I like it.
It tastes like macaroons.
There isn't enough roughage.
Add some All Bran and some prunes,

Raw carrot juice and sea salt
And a pot of yoghurt too,
Some soya and some vitamins
And then your pud will do."

It was time at last to cook it.
Just then grandad called and said
"Cow heel and tripe and faggots,
Mushy peas and eggy bread."

The Rasta in the house behind
Threw in some ganja weed.
The dog suggested Kennomeat,
The budgie gave some seed.

The pudding, as you might expect,
Had grown a bit in size.
There was far too much for Christmas
To the Mattocks's surprise.

They kept a bit and put the rest
Outside the door one day.
A fleet of trucks with yellow skips
Then took it all away.

When you see a building site
Where concrete's being laid,
Hold your nose and look at it
And think just how it's made.

There's scaffolding and aggregate
And shuttering of wood
And the ready-mix is pouring in
The Mattocks' Christmas pud.

Betty Maloney

Betty Maloney
Was very short-sighted.
She'd cut her friends dead
And they always felt slighted
For she was determined
She'd never disclose
That she couldn't see much
Past the end of her nose.

She'd board the first bus
That she saw come along
Then wonder why Parliament
Square looked all wrong,
Until the conductor,
Whose temper was short,
Said, "Another ten pence, ma'am,
We're in Earl's Court."

She'd happily pour out
A whisky and tonic,
Expect to hear songs
From the New Philarmonic,
Grope for the phone
When afloat on the Broads
Or ask where the goalposts
Had got to at Lord's.

Last Friday she went
To the Zoo, where she fell
In the pit, so she thought,
Of the Thompson's gazelle.
This delicate creature
Could do her no harm
So she held out a sandwich
And turned on her charm.

But when it came closer
It wasn't the least
Like a Thompson's or springbok
Or similar beast.
"Good tiger," she said
With a hint of a frown.
But it wasn't that good
And it swallowed her down.

Mrs Wadkin's Revenge

Mrs Wadkin's vulture
Was a vicious thing called Vic,
So ugly that the sight of him
Would almost make you sick.

He perched upon her chimney
With such evil in his eye
That the gave the heeby-jeebies
To every passer-by.

She bought the threadbare creature
In a circus surplus sale
With a schizophrenic camel
And a lion without a tail.

She kept them in her garden shed,
Apart, that is, from Vic
(A bird who, I should also add,
Was bald, diseased and thick).

And when she went a-dining out
In restaurant or hotel
She asked them for a vulture bag
To feed her vulture well.

She fed him up on rotting scraps
Of other people's pets
Which she lifted from the dustbin
When she visited the vet's.

She then embarked on training him
With recognition charts
So he should know at just a glance
An owl and all its parts.

To tell a sparrow from an owl
Was much too much for Vic
(A sort of flying zombie,
A brainless airborne brick).

She shot an owl and stuffed it
And hung it on two hooks
And Vic began to think he knew
An owl just by its looks.

She reinforced the platform
That she'd built him up on high.
She then climbed up to join him
And they sat and scanned the sky.

She scoured the sky for Trumpington
But all to no avail,
While Vic the thick, sick vulture sat
And preened his mangy tail.

Suddenly one morning
There appeared far in the west
A flying dark and tiny speck
Which wasn't like the rest.

I knew that it was Trumpington
Returning to my loo
So I rushed into the garden
To see what I could do.

Vic was sitting sullenly
Examining a zit
When Mrs Wadkin nudged him
And told him "This is it!"

He took precious little notice.
She bashed him on the beak.
He blinked a bleary stare at her.
His brain began to creak.

Trumpers circled warily.
Vic began to stir.
He stretched a leg and then a wing.
His brain began to whirr.

And suddenly he thought he knew
In a vulture sort of way,
What Wadkindom required of him
Upon that fateful day.

He thought a bit and flapped a bit,
Then shot into the sky,
A tatty interceptor
With murder in his eye.

He levelled out when he had reached
Some twenty thousand feet.
He'd overshot by miles,
But he thought "That's pretty neat!

That owl will think I'm stupid
And all I've got to do
Is close my wings and drop on him.
Tonight it's Trumpers stew!"

Mrs Wadkin on her roof
Was fingering her gun.
"Beware!" I shouted, "Trumpington!
The vulture in the sun!"

The vulture's wings were folded.
He was dropping like a brick.
Trumpers flew oblivious.
I hoped it was a trick.

Then he saw Vic coming.
He made a sudden swerve.
Vic came whistling onwards
With a grim and mindless verve.

Trumpers did a loop-the-loop
And ended underneath
The spot where Vic had almost had
Him in his vulture teeth.

But Vic was not a Richtofen;
He failed to turn and kill,
While Mrs Wadkin trembled
With a pure sadistic thrill.

Then Trumpington began to do
A most surprising thing:
He slowed; he headed back to Vic;
He folded up each wing.

He dropped like Newton's apple.
Vic did much the same
And Trumpington came plummeting
And after him Vic came.

Trumpers headed straight towards
Old Mrs Wadkin's hat.
A kamikaze owl, I thought,
A case of titfer tat.

Eighteen inches from her head
He jinked and he was gone.
Vic just couldn't manage it.
He headed on and on.

Mrs Wadkin saw him.
She tried to turn and tripped.
With milliseconds still to spare
She stumbled and she slipped.

Vic missed by a whisker.
The chimney wasn't wide
But he got halfway down it
And then got stuck inside.

While muffled vulture curses came
From in the chimney stack
Mrs Wadkin fell right off
And landed on her back

Upon a council dustcart
Which was passing right on cue.
They scrunched her with the rubbish
And they never even knew.

Trumpers was beside himself.
I knew his heart's desire.
He was willing me to go next door
And light my neighbour's fire.

Subscribers

Victoria Press would like to thank the following advance subscribers to TRUMPINGTON THE OWL who have helped to make its publication possible. Subscribers have received copies of the books numbered as below and signed by the author.

Brenda Craddock (1-3), Elspeth Brown (4), David J Brookes (5), anon (6), Maria Burt (7-9), Graham Jenkinson (10-12), Mrs M Booth (13-14), Mrs Jackie Bogliatto (15-17), Ruth Ling (18), Mrs BM Still (19), Sarah Stevens (20), anon (21), Jonathan Blake (22), anon (23-25), Mr & Mrs JI Calcott (29-31), Mrs FJ Greer (32), Catriona Blaker and Michael Blaker (33-34), anon (35), Donald M Smith (36-38), Mrs Ann Lee (39), Elaine Bousfield (40), Cathy Pearson (41), Adrienne Fryer (42), Lizzie Shirreff (43-45), Derek Spruce (46), Mrs UV Melhuish (47), Hazel C McCullagh (48), Phillip Evitt and Joanna Davies (49), A Mackay Miller (50-51), Rebecca Mackay Miller (52), Thomas Mackay Miller (53), anon (54), Stephen Marquez (55-57), Jane Corsellis (58), Maggie Henriques (59), anon (60), R Salmon (61-70), Carol Lawrence (71), Celia Haddon (72), Aileen McKenzie (73), Mark Gore (74), Sarah and Adrian Williams (75), Robin and Sally Lovell (76), WNL Haynes (77), June Davies (78), Roger N Elms (79-84), Fran Taylor (85-94), JC Richardson (95-96), Dr & Mrs GR Kershaw (97), Mrs Carol M Carsley (98), anon (99), BM Anderson (100), Mrs JR Taylor (101-103), anon (104), Hamilton (105), anon (106-107), Timothy Benthall (108-110), Mrs CH Towlson (111), Richard Stilgoe (112-113), Mrs VH Higgins (114), Dr GL Ward (115-117), anon (118), anon (119), Peter L Ward (120), Mary B Rix (121), anon (122), Mrs Catherine Curtis (123), Mrs GP Beck (124), Celia Smith (125), Miss N Welsh (126), Michael Collins (127), Chris Streatfeild (128), Mrs Angela Joyce (129-132), Daphne Hay (133), Neville Taylor and Maggie Taylor (134), Mrs P Feakes (135), Sabine Wagner (136-138), J Dees (139-141), anon (142), Irene Gladstone (143), Zosia Fenna (144), anon (145), Jacqueline Walkington (146), Jeanine and Michael Barton (147), Ms Lesley South (148-149), anon (150), anon (151), anon (152), Liz Harvey (153-155), Philip May (156), Valerie Garrett (157), Jane Perrin (158), Mrs EA Brown (159), Angela Lee (160-161), Dr Michael Orr (162), Maureen Norris (163), anon (164), Dr Derek Hope (165).